LIVE IT:
INTEGRITY

ROBERT WALKER

Crabtree Publishing Company
www.crabtreebooks.com

Author: Robert Walker
Coordinating editor: Bonnie Dobkin
Publishing plan research and development:
    Sean Charlebois, Reagan Miller
    Crabtree Publishing Company
Editor: Reagan Miller
Proofreader: Crystal Sikkens
Editorial director: Kathy Middleton
Production coordinator: Margaret Salter
Prepress technician: Margaret Salter

Logo design: Samantha Crabtree
Project Manager: Santosh Vasudevan (Q2AMEDIA)
Art Direction: Rahul Dhiman (Q2AMEDIA)
Design: Neha Kaul (Q2AMEDIA)
Illustrations: Q2AMEDIA
Front Cover: Nelson Mandela fought to free his country,
    South Africa, from apartheid and went on to become
    its president.
Title Page: Nelson Mandela is finally freed after 27 years
    in prison.

Library and Archives Canada Cataloguing in Publication

Walker, Robert, 1980-
    Live it: integrity / Robert Walker.

(Crabtree character sketches)
Includes index.
ISBN 978-0-7787-4886-1 (bound).--ISBN 978-0-7787-4919-6 (pbk.)

    1. Integrity--Juvenile literature. 2. Biography--Juvenile literature.
I. Title. II. Title: Integrity. III. Series: Crabtree character sketches

BJ1533.I58W34 2010   j179'.9   C2009-905526-0

Library of Congress Cataloging-in-Publication Data

Walker, Robert, 1980-
    Live it. Integrity / Robert Walker.
        p. cm. -- (Crabtree character sketches)
    Includes index.
    ISBN 978-0-7787-4919-6 (pbk. : alk. paper) -- ISBN 978-0-7787-4886-1
(reinforced library binding : alk. paper)
    1. Integrity--Juvenile literature. 2. Conduct of life--Juvenile literature.
I. Title. II. Title: Integrity. III. Series.

    BJ1533.I58W35 2010
    179'.9--dc22
                                                        2009036789

Crabtree Publishing Company

Printed in the USA/122009/BG20090930

www.crabtreebooks.com   1-800-387-7650

Published in Canada
Crabtree Publishing
616 Welland Ave.
St. Catharines, ON
L2M 5V6

Published in the United States
Crabtree Publishing
PMB 59051
350 Fifth Avenue, 59th Floor
New York, New York 10118

Published in the United Kingdom
Crabtree Publishing
Maritime House
Basin Road North, Hove
BN41 1WR

Published in Australia
Crabtree Publishing
386 Mt. Alexander Rd.
Ascot Vale (Melbourne)
VIC 3032

CONTENTS

WHAT IS INTEGRITY?

"SHE'S A PERSON OF INTEGRITY." YOU MAY HAVE HEARD PEOPLE SAY SOMETHING LIKE THIS. BUT WHAT IS INTEGRITY? WOULD YOU RECOGNIZE IT IF YOU SAW IT?

INTEGRITY MEANS DOING WHAT YOU SAY YOU'RE GOING TO DO AND STAYING TRUE TO YOUR BELIEFS. YOU'RE ABOUT TO MEET SEVERAL MEN AND WOMEN WHO BECAME SYMBOLS OF INTEGRITY TO EVERYONE THEY MET.

NELSON MANDELA
FORMER PRESIDENT OF SOUTH AFRICA

NELLIE McCLUNG
WOMEN'S RIGHTS *ACTIVIST*

ELEANOR ROOSEVELT
FORMER FIRST LADY OF THE UNITED STATES

JOHN MCCAIN
UNITED STATES SENATOR

MUHAMMAD ALI
THREE-TIME WORLD HEAVYWEIGHT CHAMPION

LILLIAN HELLMAN
WRITER

INTEGRITY AND SACRIFICES

NELSON MANDELA

WHO IS HE?
FORMER SOUTH AFRICAN PRESIDENT

WHY HIM?
HE FOUGHT TO END *APARTHEID* IN SOUTH AFRICA.

NELSON MANDELA FOUGHT FOR EQUAL RIGHTS FOR BLACK SOUTH AFRICANS. HE BELIEVED SO MUCH IN THE CAUSE THAT HE WAS WILLING TO GIVE UP HIS OWN FREEDOM.

IN THE 1950S, NELSON WAS A BUSY YOUNG LAWYER IN JOHANNESBURG, SOUTH AFRICA. HE OPENED THE FIRST ALL-BLACK LAW PRACTICE IN THE CITY.

PLEASE SIT DOWN. I'M SURE I CAN HELP YOU.

NELSON WAS ALSO AN IMPORTANT MEMBER OF THE *AFRICAN NATIONAL CONGRESS* (ANC). THIS GROUP WORKED TO END APARTHEID IN SOUTH AFRICA.

WE ARE NOT AGAINST ANY GROUP OF PEOPLE OR ANY GOVERNMENT. WE ARE OPPOSING A SYSTEM WHICH HAS FOR YEARS KEPT A VAST SECTION OF PEOPLE IN *BONDAGE.**

*ACTUAL QUOTE

UNDER APARTHEID, WHITE PEOPLE RAN THE COUNTRY EVEN THOUGH THEY WERE A SMALL *MINORITY*.

PEOPLE OF COLOR EARN LESS MONEY. WE HAVE TO USE SEPARATE BUSES AND SCHOOLS. WE HAVE TO CARRY PASSES TO MOVE AROUND OUR OWN COUNTRY. IT'S NOT RIGHT!

EVENTUALLY, THE ALL-WHITE GOVERNMENT BANNED THE ANC.

IN 1961, NELSON HELPED FORM *UMKHONTO WE SIZWE*, OR "SPEAR OF THE NATION." THIS GROUP COMMITTED ACTS OF *SABOTAGE* TO FIGHT APARTHEID.

IT MUST BE THOSE REBELS AGAIN. THEY'RE ATTACKING GOVERNMENT BUILDINGS, DESTROYING POWER STATIONS...

NELSON WAS ARRESTED AND GIVEN A LIFE SENTENCE AT ROBBEN ISLAND PRISON.

I HAVE CHERISHED THE IDEAL OF A DEMOCRATIC AND FREE SOCIETY IN WHICH ALL PERSONS LIVE IN HARMONY AND WITH EQUAL OPPORTUNITIES.... IT IS AN IDEAL FOR WHICH I AM PREPARED TO DIE.*

*ACTUAL QUOTE

LIFE AT THE PRISON WAS HARD.

WE BREAK OUR BACKS ALL DAY IN THIS QUARRY. AND THE FOOD— IT'S ALMOST TOO BAD TO EAT!

AND SOME OF THE GUARDS ARE MORE DANGEROUS THAN ANY OF THE PRISONERS.

OUTSIDE THE PRISON, APARTHEID—AND THE VIOLENCE—CONTINUED.

7

IN 1985, AFTER MANDELA HAD BEEN IN JAIL FOR ALMOST TWENTY YEARS. SOUTH AFRICAN PRIME MINISTER P.W. BOTHA OFFERED TO RELEASE HIM.

...BUT ONLY IF HE SWEARS TO GIVE UP VIOLENT *RESISTANCE*.

NELSON WILL NEVER AGREE TO THAT.

GOOD. THEN THE WORLD WILL SEE HOW DANGEROUS HE IS, AND WHY WE HAD HIM LOCKED UP IN THE FIRST PLACE.

NELSON WROTE HIS RESPONSE TO BOTHA THAT NIGHT.

THIS WILL BE THE FIRST TIME IN YEARS MY WORDS WILL BE HEARD IN PUBLIC. I NEED TO MAKE THEM COUNT.

NELSON'S DAUGHTER ZINDZI READ NELSON'S RESPONSE TO A CROWD OF THOUSANDS AT AN ANTI-APARTHEID RALLY IN JOHANNESBURG.

"TOO MANY HAVE SUFFERED FOR THE LOVE OF FREEDOM. I OWE IT TO THEIR WIDOWS, TO THEIR ORPHANS, TO THEIR MOTHERS, AND TO THEIR FATHERS WHO HAVE GRIEVED AND WEPT FOR THEM... I CANNOT SELL MY *BIRTHRIGHT*, NOR AM I PREPARED TO SELL THE BIRTHRIGHT OF THE PEOPLE, TO BE FREE.... YOUR FREEDOM AND MINE CANNOT BE SEPARATED."*

*ACTUAL QUOTE

NELSON TURNED DOWN BOTHA'S OFFER.

BUT YOU WOULD HAVE BEEN FREE, NELSON! BACK WITH YOUR FRIENDS AND FAMILY AFTER 20 YEARS!

EVEN IF I TOOK THE DEAL, WE WOULD ALL STILL BE PRISONERS OF APARTHEID.

NELSON WAS FINALLY FREED *UNCONDITIONALLY* IN 1990, AFTER **27** YEARS IN PRISON. HE WENT ON TO BECOME PRESIDENT OF SOUTH AFRICA, ENDING APARTHEID FOR GOOD.

I STAND BEFORE YOU NOT AS A PROPHET, BUT AS A HUMBLE SERVANT OF YOU, THE PEOPLE. YOUR TIRELESS AND HEROIC SACRIFICES HAVE MADE IT POSSIBLE FOR ME TO BE HERE TODAY.*

NELSON BELIEVED SO MUCH IN THE FIGHT TO END APARTHEID THAT HE WAS WILLING TO GIVE UP HIS LIFE AND HIS FREEDOM. FEW PEOPLE WOULD EVER HAVE SHOWN SO MUCH INTEGRITY.

WHAT WOULD YOU DO IN THE FACE OF INEQUALITY? WHAT WOULD YOU RISK?

WHAT WOULD YOU DO?

A GROUP OF KIDS AT YOUR SCHOOL HAS TAKEN CONTROL OF THE CAFETERIA. THEY DECIDE WHO SITS WHERE, AND WHO CAN SIT WITH WHOM. IF THEY DON'T LIKE YOU OR THINK YOU'RE NOT IMPORTANT, THEN YOU'RE SENT TO ONE OF THE TABLES WHERE THE UNPOPULAR KIDS SIT.

YOU KNOW THIS ISN'T FAIR, BUT CROSSING THOSE KIDS COULD LEAD TO TROUBLE. WHAT DO YOU DO?

*ACTUAL QUOTE

INTEGRITY AND WOMEN'S RIGHTS

NELLIE MCCLUNG

WHO IS SHE?
WOMEN'S RIGHTS ACTIVIST

WHY HER?
SHE HELPED GET VOTING RIGHTS FOR WOMEN IN CANADA.

NOT THAT LONG AGO, WOMEN IN NORTH AMERICA HAD FEW RIGHTS. THEY RARELY HAD JOBS, AND A WIFE WAS SEEN AS HER HUSBAND'S PROPERTY. WOMEN WERE ALSO NOT ALLOWED TO VOTE.

IN THE EARLY *1900s*, NELLIE AND HER FRIENDS WORKED TO CHANGE ALL THAT.

NELLIE MCCLUNG LIVED WITH HER HUSBAND AND FIVE CHILDREN IN WINNIPEG, MANITOBA. AT HOME, SHE WAS A LOVING WIFE AND MOTHER.

OPEN UP, HERE COMES YOUR VEGETABLES.

OPEN UP, SON.

OUTSIDE HER HOME, NELLIE FOUGHT FOR WOMEN'S RIGHTS. SHE HELPED STAGE *RALLIES* AND PROTESTS.

....WHY SHOULDN'T WE HAVE THE SAME RIGHTS AS MEN? IS A WOMAN ANY LESS OF A PERSON THAN A MAN?

CLAP

CLAP

CLAP

CLAP

NO! WOMEN ARE EQUAL TO MEN!

BUT THERE WAS ONE VERY BIG PROBLEM STANDING IN THEIR WAY—

TO ALLOW A WOMAN INTO THE WORLD OF POLITICS WOULD MEAN SHE WOULD ABANDON HER CHILDREN, AND SOCIETY AS A WHOLE WOULD SUFFER!

PROBLEMS WITH THE PREMIER WERE NOTHING NEW. SOME TIME EARLIER, NELLIE HAD TRIED TO CHANGE HIS MIND ABOUT WORKING CONDITIONS FOR WOMEN.

I'M STILL NOT SURE WHY WE'RE VISITING THIS FACTORY. I SHOULD BE IN MY OFFICE. AND YOU LADIES SHOULD BE AT HOME WITH YOUR CHILDREN.

NO, WE SHOULDN'T, PREMIER. WE CAN'T SIT COMFORTABLY AT HOME WHEN OTHER WOMEN ARE SUFFERING.

THE SMELL OF THIS PLACE!

YOU SEE, PREMIER, THESE WOMEN WORK LONG HOURS IN TERRIBLE CONDITIONS FOR LITTLE PAY. IT'S LIKE THIS AT FACTORIES ALL OVER THE CITY.

I NEED AIR!

YOUR FACTORY *INSPECTOR* HAS DONE NOTHING ABOUT THIS, PREMIER. WHAT WE NEED IS A FEMALE FACTORY INSPECTOR WHO UNDERSTANDS THESE WOMEN.

A GOVERNMENT JOB IS NO PLACE FOR A WOMAN. NOW, IF YOU'LL EXCUSE ME.

LATER, NELLIE DIDN'T HAVE MUCH MORE SUCCESS WHEN SHE SPOKE WITH ROBLIN ABOUT CHANGING THE VOTING LAWS.

NICE WOMEN DON'T EVEN WANT THE VOTE, THEY WANT TO STAY AT HOME AND TAKE CARE OF THEIR FAMILIES!

THAT IS RIDICULOUS! JUST BECAUSE WE WANT THE SAME RIGHTS AS MEN DOESN'T MEAN WE'RE NOT "NICE WOMEN!"

THAT DIDN'T GO WELL. WHAT DO WE DO NOW?

ROBLIN WONT BUDGE. WE HAVE TO FIND A WAY TO SHOW PEOPLE HOW WRONG HE IS.

NELLIE WAS A TALENTED WRITER. SHE CAME UP WITH THE IDEA TO PUT ON A PLAY TO MAKE SURE THEIR MESSAGE WAS HEARD.

WE'LL PRETEND WOMEN ARE IN CHARGE OF THE GOVERNMENT, AND THAT MEN WANT THE RIGHT TO VOTE.

TELL ME AGAIN, HOW WILL THIS HELP OUR CAUSE?

YOU'LL SEE. I'M GOING TO USE ROBLIN'S OWN WORDS AGAINST HIM.

GIVE MEN THE VOTE!

MRS. ROBLIN, WE MEN DESERVE THE SAME RIGHTS...

NO SIR! TO ALLOW A MAN INTO THE WORLD OF POLITICS WOULD MEAN HE WOULD ABANDON HIS CHILDREN, AND SOCIETY AS A WHOLE WOULD SUFFER!

WHEN YOU ASK FOR THE VOTE FOR MEN, YOU ARE ASKING ME TO BREAK UP PEACEFUL, HAPPY HOMES, TO WRECK INNOCENT LIVES, AND THIS IS SOMETHING I WILL NOT DO....*

NELLIE'S PLAY WAS A GREAT SUCCESS—AND SUPPORT FOR THE **SUFFRAGE** MOVEMENT IN MANITOBA GREW.

ROBLIN RESIGNED THE FOLLOWING YEAR. THEN, IN 1916, WOMEN IN MANITOBA GOT THE RIGHT TO VOTE.

HA HA HA HA

NELLIE WOULD CONTINUE FIGHTING FOR WOMEN'S RIGHTS FOR THE REST OF HER LIFE. SHE COULD HAVE STAYED COMFORTABLY AT HOME. BUT HER INTEGRITY, HER STRONG BELIEF IN WHAT WAS RIGHT, WOULDN'T LET HER.

WOULD YOU BE WILLING TO FIGHT FOR A CAUSE, EVEN IF YOU DIDN'T HAVE TO?

WHAT WOULD YOU DO?

YOUR PARK DISTRICT HAS ALWAYS OFFERED FREE SUMMER PROGRAMS. THIS YEAR, THOUGH, THEY'VE STARTED TO CHARGE FAMILIES FOR EVERY ACTIVITY. SOME FAMILIES CAN'T AFFORD THE NEW FEES.

YOU'RE STILL ABLE TO TAKE PART IN THE PROGRAMS, BUT NOT EVERYONE IS, INCLUDING SOME OF YOUR FRIENDS. WHAT WOULD YOU DO?

*ACTUAL QUOTE

SPEAKING OUT

ELEANOR ROOSEVELT

WHO IS SHE?
FORMER FIRST LADY OF UNITED STATES; WIFE OF FRANKLIN DELANO ROOSEVELT

WHY HER?
SHE HELPED FIGHT RACIAL **DISCRIMINATION** IN AMERICA.

ELEANOR ROOSEVELT WORKED ALL HER LIFE FOR SOCIAL JUSTICE. SHE SUPPORTED WOMEN'S RIGHTS, FOUGHT RACISM, AND HELPED THOSE IN NEED.

SHE WAS ALSO WILLING TO RISK HER OWN REPUTATION TO STAND UP FOR WHAT SHE THOUGHT WAS RIGHT.

IN 1932, FRANKLIN DELANO ROOSEVELT WAS ELECTED PRESIDENT OF THE UNITED STATES.

BECAUSE HE WAS PARTIALLY DISABLED DUE TO POLIO, ELEANOR BECAME AN IMPORTANT PARTNER IN HIS WORK.

DURING THE **GREAT DEPRESSION**, ELEANOR TRAVELED ACROSS THE COUNTRY TO SEE WHAT AMERICANS NEEDED.

I WORKED HARD ALL MY LIFE. BUT NOW WE DON'T HAVE ANYTHING.

WHEN HUNGRY, UNEMPLOYED VETERANS OF WORLD WAR I CAME TO WASHINGTON TO PROTEST, IT WAS ELEANOR WHO MET WITH THEM.

NO FIRST LADY BEFORE ELEANOR HAD HELD PRESS CONFERENCES. SHE USUALLY INVITED ONLY FEMALE REPORTERS, HOPING TO ENCOURAGE NEWSPAPERS TO HIRE MORE WOMEN.

....NOW, IF ANYONE HAS ANY QUESTIONS? YES, MISS SPENCER, FROM THE CHRONICLE?

THANK YOU. WHAT ARE YOUR THOUGHTS ON THE INCIDENT INVOLVING MARIAN ANDERSON AND THE *DAR*—THE *DAUGHTERS OF THE AMERICAN REVOLUTION?*

MARIAN ANDERSON WAS A FAMOUS SINGER WHO PERFORMED ACROSS THE UNITED STATES AND EUROPE.

AVE MARIA...

BUT WHEN SHE TRIED TO BOOK A PERFORMANCE AT CONSTITUTION HALL IN WASHINGTON...

THE DAR SAID "NO?"

WELL, THEY OWN CONSTITUTION HALL, AND THEY STILL HAVE A STRICT "NO BLACK PERFORMERS" POLICY.

HOW CAN A GROUP DEDICATED TO PROMOTING PATRIOTISM AND EDUCATION BEHAVE THIS WAY?

15

MARIAN'S FANS WERE OUTRAGED. THEY FLOODED THE NEWSPAPERS WITH ANGRY LETTERS.

WHAT ARE YOU THINKING, ELEANOR? AFTER ALL, YOU'RE A MEMBER OF THE DAR.

I KNOW. I KNOW! HERE I AM, FIGHTING SEGREGATION, AND A GROUP I BELONG TO WON'T LET A BLACK WOMAN SING AT THEIR HALL!

WHATEVER I DO WILL ANGER PEOPLE, FRANKLIN. BUT I HAVE TO DO WHAT'S RIGHT.

FIRST, ELEANOR WROTE TO MRS. HENRY M. ROBERT, JR., THE PRESIDENT OF THE DAR.

MY DEAR MRS. HENRY M. ROBERT, JR..... I AM IN COMPLETE DISAGREEMENT WITH THE ATTITUDE TAKEN IN REFUSING CONSTITUTION HALL TO A GREAT ARTIST...

"I FEEL OBLIGED TO SEND IN TO YOU MY RESIGNATION. YOU HAD AN OPPORTUNITY TO LEAD IN AN **ENLIGHTENED** WAY, AND IT SEEMS TO ME THAT YOUR ORGANIZATION HAS FAILED."*

*ACTUAL QUOTE

I HEARD ABOUT YOUR RESIGNATION, MRS. ROOSEVELT. THANK YOU SO MUCH FOR YOUR SUPPORT.

THERE'S NO NEED TO THANK ME, MISS ANDERSON. THE DAR WAS WRONG. AND HERE'S WHAT I'D LIKE TO DO...

ELEANOR ORGANIZED A CONCERT FOR MARIAN AT THE LINCOLN MEMORIAL ON EASTER SUNDAY, 1939. A CROWD OF ALMOST 75,000 PEOPLE CAME TO HEAR HER SING.

....SWEET LAND OF LIBERTY...

MARIAN'S CONCERT WAS A MILESTONE IN THE FIGHT TO END DISCRIMINATION. A FEW MONTHS LATER, ELEANOR INVITED HER TO SING AT THE WHITE HOUSE..

ELEANOR ROOSEVELT WAS AN AMAZING WOMAN! SHE CARED MORE ABOUT DOING WHAT WAS RIGHT THAN IN PLAYING IT SAFE.

WHAT IF DOING THE RIGHT THING COULD COST YOU SOMETHING IMPORTANT? WOULD YOU STILL DO IT?

WHAT WOULD YOU DO?

YOUR SOCCER COACH TREATS SOME OF THE WEAKER KIDS ON THE TEAM BADLY. THE COACH YELLS AT THEM WHEN THEY MAKE A MISTAKE, AND MAKES FUN OF THEM IF THEY GET UPSET.

YOU WANT TO STAND UP FOR THOSE KIDS, BUT IF YOU DO, THE COACH MIGHT TURN AGAINST YOU. WHAT WOULD YOU DO?

INTEGRITY IN DARKEST TIMES

JOHN MCCAIN

WHO IS HE?
UNITED STATES SENATOR

WHY HIM?
HE RESISTED HIS CAPTORS AS A PRISONER OF WAR.

AS A PRISONER OF WAR, JOHN MCCAIN WAS BEATEN, TORTURED, AND STARVED. YET HE HELD FIRM TO HIS BELIEFS—THOUGH FEW OTHER PEOPLE COULD HAVE.

READ ON TO SEE AN EXAMPLE OF REAL INTEGRITY IN ACTION.

JOHN MCCAIN WAS A UNITED STATES PILOT WHO FOUGHT IN THE VIETNAM WAR.

THIS WAR WAS FOUGHT BETWEEN NORTH VIETNAM—A COMMUNIST COUNTRY—AND SOUTH VIETNAM, A COUNTRY SUPPORTED BY THE U.S.A.

IN 1967, JOHN WAS CHOSEN FOR A DANGEROUS MISSION DEEP INSIDE ENEMY TERRITORY.

AS JOHN NEARED HIS TARGET, HIS PLANE WAS HIT BY AN ENEMY MISSILE.

HE EJECTED BEFORE THE PLANE WENT DOWN.

JOHN LANDED IN A LAKE. HE HAD TWO BROKEN ARMS AND A BROKEN LEG.

VILLAGERS PULLED HIM OUT AND HANDED HIM OVER TO THE NORTH VIETNAMESE ARMY. HE WAS NOW A PRISONER OF WAR, OR POW.

AT FIRST, JOHN WAS REFUSED MEDICAL CARE. THEN THE NORTH VIETNAMESE OFFICIALS LEARNED HIS FATHER WAS AN IMPORTANT MEMBER OF THE UNITED STATES NAVY.

A FRENCH TV REPORTER IS COMING TO SEE YOU. YOU TELL HIM YOU ARE SORRY FOR ATTACKING US, AND GRATEFUL THAT WE SAVED YOU.

SO YOU CAN USE IT IN YOUR **PROPAGANDA?** NO. I WON'T SAY THAT.

HIS CAPTORS WERE ANGRY AT HIS REFUSAL AND SENT HIM TO A PRISON CAMP.

I DON'T THINK HE'S GOING TO MAKE IT.

ME NEITHER. THEY SET HIS BONES CROOKED, AND HE'S BURNING WITH FEVER.

BUT JOHN DID SURVIVE. HE WAS KEPT ALONE IN A WINDOWLESS CELL FOR TWO YEARS.

TAP TAP

TAP TAP

HIS ONLY CONTACT WITH OTHERS WAS THROUGH MESSAGES TAPPED ON THE WALL.

WHAT?!? WHY?

BECAUSE THERE ARE PRISONERS WHO'VE BEEN HERE LONGER THAN ME. THEY GO HOME BEFORE I DO. IF I LET YOU SEND ME HOME FIRST, IT MEANS SOMEONE ELSE STAYS HERE INSTEAD. THE LAST THING I WANT TO DO IS HELP YOU HURT ANOTHER SOLDIER.

JOHN NEVER ACCEPTED THEIR OFFER. HE STAYED A PRISONER OF WAR FOR OVER FIVE YEARS. HE WAS FINALLY RELEASED IN 1973.

MCCAIN WENT ON TO A RESPECTED CAREER IN POLITICS. HE BROUGHT WITH HIM THE SAME INTEGRITY HE DISPLAYED AS A PRISONER OF WAR.

IT'S HARD TO IMAGINE A TOUGHER PLACE TO HANG ON TO YOUR INTEGRITY THAN A PRISON CAMP. BUT JOHN MCCAIN REMAINED TRUE TO HIS COUNTRY AND TO HIS FELLOW SOLDIERS.

HOW WELL DO YOU THINK YOU'D DO IF YOUR INTEGRITY WAS TESTED?

WHAT WOULD YOU DO?

IMAGINE YOUR TOWN HAS BEEN HIT BY A DISASTER. RELIEF ORGANIZATIONS ARE PROVIDING FOOD AND SUPPLIES TO THE FAMILIES THAT NEED IT MOST.

YOUR PARENTS ARE WELL KNOWN IN THE COMMUNITY, AND SOMEONE OFFERS TO PUT YOUR NAME AT THE TOP OF THIS LIST OF PEOPLE WHO WILL RECEIVE AID. WHAT WOULD YOU SAY TO YOUR PARENTS?

STAYING TRUE TO YOUR BELIEFS

MUHAMMAD ALI

WHO IS HE?
THREE-TIME WORLD
HEAVYWEIGHT CHAMPION

WHY HIM?
HE RISKED HIS CAREER TO STAY
TRUE TO HIS BELIEFS.

MUHAMMAD ALI—ONCE KNOWN AS CASSIUS CLAY—IS A BOXING LEGEND. IN FACT, SPORTS ILLUSTRATED NAMED HIM SPORTSMAN OF THE CENTURY IN 1999.

ALI WAS ALSO ADMIRED FOR HIS INTEGRITY. CHECK OUT A CHOICE HE MADE THAT PUT HIS ENTIRE CAREER ON THE LINE.

WHEN HE WAS 12 YEARS OLD, CASSIUS CLAY HAD HIS NEW RED BIKE STOLEN.

I'M GOING TO GET WHOEVER TOOK IT! I'M GOING TO FIND 'EM AND—

THE GUY WHO RUNS THE BOXING GYM DOWNSTAIRS IS A POLICE OFFICER. WHY NOT TALK TO HIM, FIRST?

CASSIUS TOLD OFFICER JOE MARTIN ABOUT HIS BIKE.

WHEN I FIND WHO TOOK MY BIKE I'M GOING TO WHUP 'EM GOOD!

DO YOU KNOW HOW TO FIGHT, KID?

NO.

WELL, MAYBE WE SHOULD TEACH YOU TO FIGHT BEFORE YOU TRY TO "WHUP" ANYONE.

CASSIUS STARTED TRAINING AT THE GYM EVERY DAY.

CASSIUS WAS A NATURAL BOXER. BY THE TIME HE WAS 18, HE HAD WON 100 FIGHTS AND LOST ONLY EIGHT.

IN 1960, HE REPRESENTED THE UNITED STATES AT THE SUMMER OLYMPICS IN ROME.

... AND TAKING HOME THE GOLD MEDAL, CASSIUS CLAY OF THE UNITED STATES OF AMERICA.

THEN, IN 1964, CASSIUS DEFEATED CHAMP SONNY LISTON TO WIN THE WORLD HEAVYWEIGHT BOXING CHAMPIONSHIP.

THE WINNER AND NEW HEAVYWEIGHT CHAMPION OF THE WORLD— CASSIUS CLAY!

AFTER THE LISTON FIGHT, CASSIUS ANNOUNCED HE WAS JOINING THE **NATION OF ISLAM**, AN ALL-BLACK RELIGIOUS GROUP.

AS A SIGN OF RESPECT FOR MY NEW FAITH, I AM CHANGING MY NAME TO MUHAMMED ALI.

ALI MARRIED AND BEGAN A FAMILY. THINGS WENT WELL UNTIL 1967. THAT'S WHEN ALI WAS **DRAFTED** TO FIGHT IN THE VIETNAM WAR.

BUT YOU CAN'T SERVE IN THE MILITARY. YOU'RE A **MUSLIM**.

IT'S MORE THAN THAT. I ALREADY ANNOUNCED THAT I'M A **CONSCIENTIOUS OBJECTOR**, TOO. BUT THE GOVERNMENT DOESN'T SEEM TO CARE.

ALI TOLD THE ARMY HE WOULD NOT REPORT FOR DUTY—EVEN THOUGH THAT MEANT HE COULD GO TO JAIL.

MR. ALI! WHY HAVE YOU REFUSED YOUR DRAFT ORDER?

WAR IS AGAINST THE TEACHINGS OF THE HOLY *QUR'AN*. WE ARE NOT SUPPOSED TO TAKE PART IN ... WARS UNLESS DECLARED BY *ALLAH* OR THE *MESSENGER*.*

*ACTUAL QUOTE

YOU HAVE BEEN FOUND GUILTY OF REFUSAL TO BE DRAFTED INTO THE ARMED SERVICES. YOU ARE HEREBY SENTENCED TO FIVE YEARS IN PRISON, AND A $10,000 FINE.

ALI WAS STRIPPED OF HIS BOXING TITLE, AND BANNED FROM PROFESSIONAL BOXING.

MEANWHILE, ALI'S FRIENDS AND LAWYERS TRIED TO FIND WAYS TO KEEP HIM OUT OF PRISON.

WHAT IF YOU JOINED THE NATIONAL GUARD? THEN YOU COULD BE IN THE ARMY, BUT NOT HAVE TO FIGHT.

OR WHAT IF YOU JOIN, BUT ONLY HAVE TO ENTERTAIN THE TROOPS BY BOXING?

MANY PEOPLE ATTACKED ALI FOR HIS DECISION NOT TO FIGHT. EVEN SOME MEMBERS OF THE BLACK COMMUNITY FELT HE WAS AN "EMBARRASSMENT."

I'M GRATEFUL FOR WHAT YOU ALL ARE TRYING TO DO. BUT I CAN'T SUPPORT THIS WAR IN ANY WAY. I CAN'T BACK DOWN.

...UT ALI STOOD HIS GROUND AND CONTINUED TO SPEAK OUT AGAINST THE WAR.

IN 1970, THE SUPREME COURT RULED IN ALI'S FAVOR, AND HE RETURNED TO BOXING. HE WOULD WIN BACK HIS CHAMPIONSHIP TITLE, BEATING GEORGE FOREMAN IN ZAIRE, AFRICA.

WHY SHOULD THEY ASK ME TO PUT ON A UNIFORM AND DROP BOMBS AND BULLETS ON BROWN PEOPLE IN VIETNAM, WHILE ... NEGRO PEOPLE IN LOUISVILLE ARE TREATED LIKE DOGS?*

*ACTUAL QUOTE

HIS APPEAL LASTED FOUR YEARS. BANNED FROM BOXING, HE LOST MILLIONS OF DOLLARS IN EARNINGS. BUT HE NEVER REGRETTED HIS DECISION.

ALI RISKED HIS CAREER TO STAND UP FOR WHAT HE BELIEVED IN! OTHER PEOPLE THOUGHT HE WAS WRONG, BUT ALI SHOWED INTEGRITY BY DOING WHAT HE FELT WAS RIGHT.

NOW, LET'S SEE WHAT YOU WOULD DO IN A SIMILAR SITUATION.

WHAT WOULD YOU DO?

YOUR SCIENCE TEACHER HAS JUST ANNOUNCED THAT THE CLASS WILL BE DISSECTING FROGS IN CLASS. YOU'RE UPSET BECAUSE YOU BELIEVE STRONGLY THAT EXPERIMENTING ON ANIMALS IS WRONG. YOU RAISE YOUR HAND AND SAY SO.

"YOU DON'T HAVE TO DO THE DISSECTION YOURSELF, THEN," SAYS YOUR TEACHER. "YOU CAN JUST TAKE NOTES ON WHAT OTHERS DO."

BUT YOU DON'T THINK ANYONE SHOULD DO THESE EXPERIMENTS. WHAT DO YOU SAY NOW?

REFUSING TO TURN ON OTHERS

LILLIAN HELLMAN

WHO IS SHE?
AN AMERICAN PLAYWRIGHT

WHY HER?
SHE WOULDN'T TURN AGAINST HER FELLOW ARTISTS.

IN THE *1940S*, THE UNITED STATES BEGAN TO FEAR THE SPREAD OF **COMMUNISM.** PEOPLE WHO SUPPORTED COMMUNIST IDEAS IN ANY WAY WERE CONSIDERED TRAITORS.

IN 1947, THE U.S. GOVERNMENT WENT ON THE HUNT FOR COMMUNISTS IN HOLLYWOOD, AND LILLIAN HELLMAN FOUND HERSELF CAUGHT IN THEIR SIGHTS!

IN 1947, THE *HOUSE UN-AMERICAN ACTIVITIES COMMITTEE* (HUAC) BEGAN TO HOLD HEARINGS TO SEARCH OUT COMMUNISTS IN THE MOTION PICTURE INDUSTRY.

WE INTEND TO FIND ALL COMMUNISTS AMONG US BEFORE THEY CAN HARM OUR COUNTRY. ARE YOU NOW, OR HAVE YOU EVER BEEN, A MEMBER OF THE COMMUNIST PARTY?

NO.

WITNESSES WERE ALSO ASKED TO "NAME NAMES"—TO TURN IN OTHER PEOPLE.

THEN DO YOU KNOW OF ANYONE WHO IS A MEMBER OF THE COMMUNIST PARTY?

NO. AND I CERTAINLY WOULDN'T TELL YOU IF I DID.

BUT SOME FIRMLY REFUSED TO COOPERATE.

THE BIG MOVIE STUDIOS WORRIED THAT THEY COULD GET IN TROUBLE IF THEY HIRED PEOPLE THAT HUAC SUSPECTED. THEY LOOKED FOR WAYS TO PROTECT THEMSELVES.

LILLIAN, I HEAR THE STUDIOS ARE **BLACKLISTING** WRITERS, DIRECTORS, ACTORS—ANYONE WHO WON'T COOPERATE WITH HUAC.

THIS IS TERRIBLE! HUAC DOESN'T EVEN HAVE PROOF THAT HALF OF THE PEOPLE THEY SAY ARE COMMUNISTS REALLY ARE!

LILLIAN WAS ANGRY NOT ONLY AT HUAC, BUT AT ANYONE FROM HOLLYWOOD WHO HELPED THEM.

READ ME THE FIRST PART OF YOUR ARTICLE AGAIN, LILLIAN.

"IT WAS A WEEK OF TURNING THE HEAD IN SHAME, OF SEEING CRAVEN MEN LIE AND TATTLE..."*

WE NEED TO STAND UP TO THESE PEOPLE, DASHIELL.

*ACTUAL QUOTE

BUT THERE WAS SOMETHING LILLIAN DIDN'T KNOW.

ALRIGHT. SO WE AGREE ON LAURENCE OLIVIER FOR THE LEAD. NOW, WHO DO WE SEE PLAYING CARRIE?

LILLIAN, THE DIRECTOR'S ON THE PHONE FOR YOU.

THANKS, ANGIE, I'LL BE RIGHT BACK.

HUAC HAD ALREADY SET ITS SIGHTS ON HER.

LILLIAN? LILLIAN, ARE YOU STILL THERE? I'M SO SORRY, BUT THERE'S NOTHING I CAN DO. THE STUDIO SAYS YOU'RE OFF THE MOVIE.

BLACKLISTED IN HOLLYWOOD, LILLIAN WENT BACK TO WORKING IN THE THEATER.

THAT WAS GREAT, BRAD. LET'S TRY IT AGAIN, BUT THIS TIME, ACT MORE SURPRISED WHEN LOUISE COMES IN.

BACK IN HOLLYWOOD, THE SITUATION GOT WORSE. PEOPLE WERE TURNING ON EACH OTHER TO SAVE THEMSELVES.

SO YOU SAW MR. HILL AT HIS COMMUNIST MEETING?

YES. HE WAS THERE.

IN 1952, IT WAS LILLIAN'S TURN TO APPEAR BEFORE THE COMMITTEE. THERE WAS A CHANCE SHE COULD GET HERSELF OFF OF THE BLACKLIST—IF SHE COOPERATED.

MS. HELLMAN HAS GIVEN US A PREPARED STATEMENT. IT READS: "I AM NOT WILLING NOW, OR IN THE FUTURE, TO BRING BAD TROUBLE TO PEOPLE WHO... WERE COMPLETELY INNOCENT OF ANY TALK OR ANY ACTION THAT WAS DISLOYAL OR *SUBVERSIVE*..."*

*ACTUAL QUOTE

MISS HELLMAN, I TAKE IT YOU ARE UNWILLING TO DISCUSS WITH US PEOPLE YOU KNOW TO BE COMMUNISTS OR OF HAVING COMMUNIST TIES?

THAT'S CORRECT, SIR....TO HURT INNOCENT PEOPLE IN ORDER TO SAVE MYSELF IS, TO ME, INHUMAN AND INDECENT AND DISHONORABLE.*

*ACTUAL QUOTE

LILLIAN REFUSED TO TURN ON HER FRIENDS TO SAVE HERSELF.

MS. HELLMAN! MS. HELLMAN! WHAT ARE YOU GOING TO DO NOW?

ARE YOU A COMMUNIST?

BUT HER INTEGRITY CAME AT A COST—SHE WOULD BE BANNED FROM HOLLYWOOD FOR OVER TEN YEARS.

LILLIAN EVENTUALLY RETURNED TO HOLLYWOOD. IN 1977, A MOVIE WAS MADE ABOUT HER LIFE. LILLIAN WAS INVITED TO PRESENT AT THE ACADEMY AWARDS THAT YEAR.

IT TOOK SOME SERIOUS INTEGRITY FOR LILLIAN HELLMAN TO REFUSE TO HELP HUAC. IF YOU HAD THE CHANCE TO HELP YOURSELF BY HURTING SOMEONE ELSE, WHAT WOULD YOU DO?

I WAS ONCE UPON A TIME A RESPECTABLE MEMBER OF THIS COMMUNITY...THEN SUDDENLY...MANY OTHERS AND I WERE NO LONGER ACCEPTABLE TO THE OWNERS OF THIS INDUSTRY.

I HAVE NO REGRETS FOR THAT PERIOD.

THE CROWD GAVE LILLIAN A STANDING OVATION.

WHAT WOULD YOU DO?

A CLASSMATE'S MP3 PLAYER HAS BEEN STOLEN. SOMEONE SAW YOU BY THAT KID'S LOCKER, AND YOU GET BLAMED.

OTHER KIDS WERE STANDING NEAR YOU AT THE TIME. YOU COULD HELP YOUR CASE BY POINTING OUT THAT ONE OF THEM COULD HAVE STOLEN THE PLAYER. WOULD YOU DO THAT? HOW ELSE COULD YOU HANDLE THIS SITUATION?

WEB SITES

VISIT THE WEB SITE BELOW TO LEARN MORE ABOUT JOHN MCCAIN'S POLITICAL CAREER.

http://mccain.senate.gov/public/

THIS WEB SITE LOOKS AT THE LIFE AND TIMES OF NELSON MANDELA.

http://news.bbc.co.uk/2/hi/africa/1454208.stm

VISIT THIS SITE TO LEARN MORE ABOUT NELLIE MCCLUNG'S FIGHT FOR WOMEN'S RIGHTS.

www.cbc.ca/lifeandtimes/mcclung.html

THE MUHAMMAD ALI CENTER TELLS ABOUT THE CHAMPION'S LIFE AND CAREER.

www.alicenter.org/Pages/default.aspx

LEARN MORE ABOUT THE HOUSE UN-AMERICAN ACTIVITIES COMMITTEE.

www.nps.gov/archive/elro/glossary/huac.htm

LEARN MORE ABOUT ELEANOR ROOSEVELT, AN AMAZING FIRST LADY.

www.whitehouse.gov/about/first_ladies/eleanorroosevelt/

GLOSSARY

ACTIVIST A PERSON WHO WORKS TO CHANGE SOMETHING

AFRICAN NATIONAL CONGRESS (ANC) A SOUTH AFRICAN POLITICAL PARTY

ALLAH THE NAME MUSLIMS USE FOR GOD

APARTHEID A SYSTEM CREATED TO KEEP PEOPLE OF DIFFERENT RACES APART

BIRTHRIGHT A RIGHT OR PRIVILEGE OWED TO A PERSON

BLACKLIST A LIST OF PEOPLE TO BE MISTREATED OR IGNORED

BONDAGE KEPT LIKE A SLAVE OR PRISONER

COMMUNISM A SOCIETY WHERE ALL PROPERTY IS PUBLICLY OWNED

CONSCIENTIOUS OBJECTOR A PERSON WHO REFUSES TO SERVE IN THE ARMED FORCES BECAUSE HE OR SHE BELIEVES IT IS WRONG

DAUGHTERS OF THE AMERICAN REVOLUTION (DAR) A WOMEN'S GROUP WHOSE ANCESTORS FOUGHT IN THE AMERICAN CIVIL WAR

DISCRIMINATION TREATING PEOPLE UNFAIRLY FOR NO GOOD REASON

DRAFT A GOVERNMENT ORDER FOR PEOPLE TO JOIN THE ARMY

ENLIGHTENED VERY SMART AND FAIR

GREAT DEPRESSION A WORLDWIDE FINANCIAL CRISIS IN THE 1920S AND '30S

HOUSE UN-AMERICAN ACTIVITIES COMMITTEE (HUAC) A COMMITTEE THAT LOOKED FOR COMMUNISTS IN GOVERNMENT AND INDUSTRY

INSPECTOR SOMEONE WHO MAKES SURE RULES ARE FOLLOWED

MESSENGER MUHAMMAD, THE CENTRAL FIGURE OF THE MUSLIM RELIGION

MINORITY THE SMALLER IN NUMBER OF TWO GROUPS THAT FORM A WHOLE

MUSLIM A MEMBER OF THE RELIGION OF ISLAM

NATION OF ISLAM AN ALL-BLACK GROUP OF THE RELIGION OF ISLAM

PROPAGANDA THE SPREAD OF IDEAS, INFORMATION, OR RUMORS TO HELP OR HURT AN INSTITUTION, A CAUSE, OR A PERSON

QUR'AN A HOLY BOOK IN THE RELIGION OF ISLAM

RALLY A LARGE GROUP OF PEOPLE COMING TOGETHER TO SUPPORT A CAUSE

RESISTANCE TO FIGHT AGAINST SOMETHING

SABOTAGE TO DESTROY OR INTERFERE WITH SOMETHING

SUBVERSIVE TRYING TO WORK AGAINST A GOVERNMENT

SUFFRAGE THE RIGHT TO VOTE

UMKHONTO WE SIZWE (SPEAR OF THE NATION) MEMBERS OF THE ANC WHO USED SABOTAGE TO FIGHT APARTHEID

UNCONDITIONALLY WITHOUT RULES OR RESTRICTIONS

INDEX